KNOW YOUR SCIENCE TOOLS

LET'S USE LENSES

DENNIS LIU

PowerKiDS press.

Published in 2027 by The Rosen Publishing Group, Inc.
2544 Clinton Street, Buffalo, NY 14224

First Edition

Editor: Noah Riccardi
Book Design: Claire Vanden Branden

Photo Credits: Cover, pp. 1, 19 AstroStar/Shutterstock.com; p. 5 Komthong-Apec/Shutterstock.com; p. 7 Apolinariy/Shutterstock.com; p. 9 Feng Yu/Shutterstock.com; p. 11 Sophon Nawit/Shutterstock.com; p. 13 yogenystocker/Shutterstock.com; p. 15 Stokkete/Shutterstock.com; pp. 17, 21 PeopleImages/Shutterstock.com.

Cataloging-in-Publication Data
Names: Liu, Dennis.
Title: Let's use lenses / Dennis Liu.
Description: Buffalo, New York : PowerKids Press, 2027. | Series: Know your science tools | Includes glossary and index.
Identifiers: ISBN 9781499459630 (pbk.) | ISBN 9781499459647 (library bound) | ISBN 9781499459654 (ebook)
Subjects: LCSH: Optical instruments--Juvenile literature.
Classification: LCC QC371.4 L58 2027 | DDC 681.4--dc23

Manufactured in China

CPSIA Compliance Information: Batch #QS27PK. For Further Information contact Rosen Publishing, at 1-800-237-9932.

CONTENTS

Looking Through a Lens

A lens is a curved piece of **material** that we can see through, such as glass. Its shape can make objects look clearer, smaller, or bigger. Lenses are tools that make our lives better! Lenses work by bending light in useful ways.

About Light

Light travels as a ray. Rays of light move in a straight line. However, they bend when they pass from one material to another, such as from air to glass. This is called refraction.

Convex Lens

People can make special lenses that bend light. A convex lens curves outward. It's thickest in the middle. When light rays pass through a convex lens, they bend toward each other. They come together at a point called the **focus**.

You may have used a **magnifying** glass. It makes small objects look much larger. You can see **details** that are hard to see with just your eyes. A magnifying glass is a convex lens.

Concave Lens

Some lenses are thicker at their edges than at the middle. These are concave lenses. When light passes through a concave lens, the rays spread apart. When you look through a concave lens, objects look farther away than they are.

2 3 9
5 2
9

Movie theaters used to use **projectors** with concave lenses. A light in the projector shined through a strip of film. A concave lens made the light rays spread out and form a large picture on a screen. Some flashlights use concave lenses, too.

1:16 F 20

Close Up and Far Away

Scientists use microscopes to see very small objects. These tools use lenses and **mirrors** to help us see things we can't see with our own eyes. Microscopes are useful for studying **minerals** and many other things.

Telescopes allow us to see objects that are very far away. Some kinds use lenses to focus light from faraway objects. They form a magnified image we can see when we look into the telescope. Telescopes are important in **astronomy**.

Your Own Two Eyes

Your eyes have lenses, too! Sometimes, these lenses don't bend light rays in the right way, so objects look blurry. Contacts and eyeglasses are lenses that help people see better. We're lucky to have lenses!

GLOSSARY

astronomy: The study of stars, planets, and other objects in outer space.

details: The small parts of something.

focus: The point at which a picture is formed by a lens. Also, to bring light rays to a point.

magnifying: Making something appear larger.

material: Matter from which something is made.

minerals: Kinds of material that make up rocks.

mirrors: Pieces of glass that reflect light.

projectors: Machines that cause movies or pictures to appear on a screen.

FOR MORE INFORMATION

BOOKS

Chapman, Amy. *Light*. Buffalo, NY: Rosen Publishing, 2026.

Raij, Emily. *How Do We Use Light?* North Mankato, MN: Capstone Publishing, 2022.

WEBSITES

Britannica Kids: Optics
kids.britannica.com/kids/article/optics/390822
Read this site to learn more about the study of light.

PBS LearningMedia: Lens and Mirror Lab
tpt.pbslearningmedia.org/resource/arct15-sci-lensmirrorlab/lens-and-mirror-lab/
See how light refracts though a lens with this tool.

INDEX